GEORG BASELITZ

GEORG BASELITZ

SCULPTURE & EARLY WOODCUTS

Anthony d'Offay Gallery

FOREWORD

By the very nature of his paintings and prints – gouged, carved, sliced, cut about, turned upside down, and above all three-dimensionally conceived as his images are – it seems inevitable that Baselitz should also make sculpture. In 1979 he began an extraordinary on-going series of large wood carvings, figures and heads, the first of which was the half-reclining *Model for a Sculpture* (Museum Ludwig, Cologne). It caused a stir at the Venice Biennale of 1980 because its raised arm, which owed something to a Congo funerary doll, was mistaken for a fascist salute. The most recent high point of this sequence is *Greetings from Oslo*, 1986, Baselitz's first carving of a female figure and the central focus of this exhibition.

The contradiction between the heroic and monumental and the humble and fragmentary, which pervades all Baselitz's work, is powerfully manifest in this huge yet unpretentious object which, before he gave it a base, was once simply hung by a string round its neck from a nail in the wall of the artist's studio. This footless Nordic Venus, who began life with the attributes of both sexes, emerged from the waves of Baselitz's creation quite deliberately as a monument by default rather than design.

She is, in a sense, a head with appendages, part of the series of heads – paintings and sculptures with huge noses – which began after the artist's visit to Norway in 1986. All this figure's power seems to be focused in that head roughly brushed with red paint. Her title, as near to blowing in the wind as you can get, nevertheless indicates with precision exactly the amount of reference the work contains to Baselitz's position in the geographic, historical and cultural scheme of things – a kind of compass reading north-north-east, looking back in distant perspective to Finnish, Teutonic, Slavonic and Celtic traditions, but not without links to Picasso and African art either. A lucky fertility charm? Artist's muse? Goddess? She belongs to the same fierce ragamuffin family of archetypes Baselitz introduced into his paintings and drawings in the sixties.

In this exhibition we have surrounded her with other heads, more carved monumental fragments of human understanding, and with a series of rare early woodcuts, which complement her archetypal origins and emphasize the importance of the sculptural element in Baselitz's work. They show how Baselitz's art is first and foremost an active undertaking, requiring the participation of the whole human being, flexibility of mind, body and spirit, how every image he creates vibrates with the energy of its making, and how constant is that activity and will to change. Everything he makes is an organic fragment of a continuously growing and changing perspective.

Joseph Beuys used the digging dwarf as a metaphor for his position and search for truth and reality. George Baselitz seems to have chosen the woodcutter. Eschewing naturalism, he chips away unceasingly, breaking through to the deeper reality beneath the surface appearance of things in a way which has nothing to do with self-expression. We would like this exhibition to demonstrate that the hand which gouged out the surface of the early woodcuts, that made actual the idea of fragmentation in the paintings of the sixties, that turned the eagle and the spluttering orange-eater on their heads, is not only identical with, but enhanced by the one that wielded axe, chisel and saw, to change a tree into the image of a woman. With the glare of a lighthouse she reflects back at us what it means to be a human being at a given point in time and space.

A d'O

An interview with Georg Baselitz by Jean-Louis Froment and Jean-Marc Poinsot

Let's start with a quick autobiographical summary, and then we'll go on to the sculptures themselves.
When was it that you crossed over from East to West?

It was in 1956. My family lived in the East. I had a Communist education, like everyone else. I spent a year at the School of Fine Arts in East Berlin, then I was expelled for socio-political immaturity. I felt really crushed by that, because I thought I had really done the best I could in the GDR. There was no real prospect of working after my expulsion, which was going to mean working in a factory or a coalmine. Then, after a year, providing I had my ideas sorted out, I would have been allowed back into the school, after a sort of 'purgation'. I didn't want to cross over to West Berlin, but there was not much point in staying in the East, from my point of view. That is why I moved to West Berlin to finish my studies. Then I had my first exhibition.

This socio-political immaturity that you were accused of: can you tell us what this meant?

The East Berlin Academy did not operate like art schools in Western countries. It was a school with a very strict discipline. There were a number of subject areas and we had to work in all of them. The school had a policy of sending its students to work in industry during the vacations. This was part of the curriculum. I was told to go to Rostock, on the Baltic. So everyone went. I wanted to stay at the school and work within the school. So I stayed behind, and by the time the other students came back at the end of the vacation I had painted 50 pictures. I was accused of socio-political immaturity for painting those pictures.

My work was incomprehensible.

Can we talk about the content of that work?

I was only 18 at the time, and the knowledge I had about painting was very limited. I had never heard of abstract painting; I knew nothing of the Bauhaus. The best-known and best-thought-of painter in the GDR was Picasso. All my friends were influenced by Picasso.

Which works by Picasso did you know?

There was very little information. We had a big book in French in the library, and there had been an exhibition of Picasso lithographs. But I had never seen any original works. What interested me was Picasso's political and social position. At that time he was still thought of as a Communist living in a decadent bourgeois society. What he was doing within that decadent bourgeois society was revolutionary. But for the people in the East this position had no validity at all.

I went to West Berlin, and there the school was run by Tachists.

When you talk about Tachism, I imagine you mean the domination of art by both the French and American schools equally?

No. It was mostly the Ecole de Paris and what came after. Hartung had a very high reputation. In Germany we had Nay. My professor, Trier, was an *informel* painter himself. I set out to steep myself in this new painting. For a year I practised it intensively: I really studied it. Then I realized that it didn't suit me. I gradually withdrew from the school and worked at home; but I was still on the roll of the school. I fell out with my professor because he didn't understand what I was doing.

In postwar Germany there was no hierarchy. There was nothing, no original painting no original culture. There was the French influence; then there was more and more American influence. All the artists working here were seeing themselves in relation to French or American artists. They were dependent on them. I didn't like this at all.

Later on, going to an exhibition and looking at the catalogue, I saw what had been done in Germany up to 1933, and I didn't feel involved with German Expressionism or the Bauhaus either. I couldn't relate to it or identify with it in any way. The one thing that interested me a great deal was Dadaism, and Kurt Schwitters in particular. It has never seemed right or possible, from my point of view at least, to pursue a tendency in an academic way. You can't treat painting like a relay race. There can't be a continuous line from one thing to another. It's not possible to do a painting as one does a sum.

Without coming to any very clear conclusion on an intellectual level, I realized, with what felt like a sensation of disgust or hatred, that I must do something different. I looked for like-minded people, and found one who came from the East like me, from the same area, and who had the same problems: this was Eugen Schönebeck. Together we wrote a manifesto in 1961, *Pandämonium*. In this manifesto there is text that is really programmatic, really savage, really straight from the gut. This text has drawings with

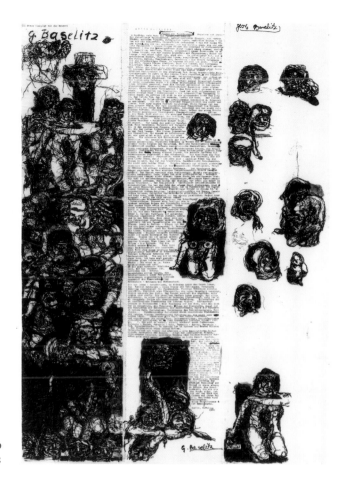

Second *Pandämonium* Manifesto
Berlin 1962

it, and it defines our position. It was this position that turned Schönebeck and myself into artists out on a limb. Then we wrote a second and third manifesto in 1962-63. The second manifesto was accompanied by an exhibition held in a space we had rented. We hung our pictures, but no one came. After this rather trying experience Schönebeck and I fell out. It wasn't that our ideas were different so much as that we were both overwrought. The situation was really desperate. We had no money left, and it was all awful.

Then I went on by myself and did the inaugural exhibition at the Michael Werner gallery in Berlin in 1963. This was a collection of my early paintings, relatively large figurative pictures. The most important one was called *Die grosse Nacht im Eimer (The Big Night in a Bucket)*. There is a German saying which says that 'it's all in the bucket', meaning that it's all in a mess, down the chute. Hence the title of my painting. On the first day everything went normally, then the *Bildzeitung* came out with a front-page article saying there was nothing in my show but filth. There was an enormous scandal and the police closed the exhibition. Then it opened again and was banned again. More and more people came. Then two paintings were confiscated. The legal battles went on for two years. The owners of the gallery, Benjamin Katz and Michael Werner, were prosecuted and found guilty along with me. We went to the highest court of appeal, and in the end we got the pictures back, but we had no money left at all.

What did those two paintings show?

One was called *The Big Night in a Bucket*, as I have said, and the other *The Naked Man.* It shows a young man with his flies open. It looks as if he is masturbating, but he isn't. It's a rather excessive, rather rude depiction of a young man. The fact that so many people came to the exhibition, and the publication of an article which was not art criticism, served to build up the issue at a time when people were not used to being confronted with images of this kind.

No one had ever shown such shocking, such provocative figure paintings in Berlin before.

The incident has its significance, and not only because of the subject...

Yes, it is important, because everything I have done has always stirred up controversy. Everything I have done has been very frank and direct, but that isn't always what the situation calls for.

So a figure painting could be more shocking than an abstract?

At that time the situation in Germany was very different from the French or American situation. All the people who had worked as painters, sculptors or writers from the turn of the century onwards had gone. They had all emigrated. They had left Germany. Our dependence on the USA and France was very strong, very important, right up to very recently. What I was doing was utterly different. This led to a lot of misunderstandings, because what I was doing was not at all what people expected. They used to say that my works were anachronistic, that they were retrograde, that I was interested in things that had been finished and done with long before. But that wasn't my problem. My intention was to illustrate my own position with the aid of a picture, and to do so in the strongest and clearest way possible. This is what happens in the picture called *The Big Night in a Bucket.* It was an act of aggression, just like the sculptures I am doing now.

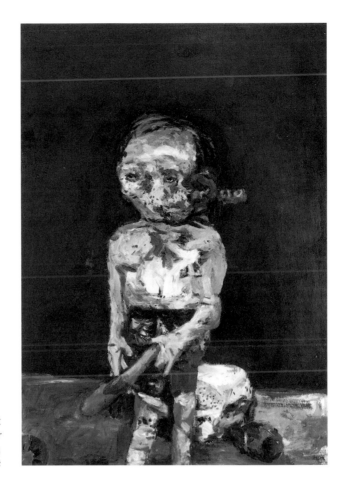

The Big Night in a Bucket
Die grosse Nacht im Eimer
1962/3
Museum Ludwig, Cologne

Then there were periods when I used my painting to deal with purely intellectual issues, which was not the case at the beginning. It was not fair to talk about anachronisms, because the pictures I painted, my figurative paintings, were things that I really invented myself. It was not that they set out to distance themselves from the model, from nature; they were genuine inventions. Over the years there have been many breaks in the continuity of my work. I have gone back to zero very many times. This has never led me to destroy what I had done before. I have always accepted it. And now that many years have passed, the works we have been talking about, such as *The Big Night in a Bucket,* really belong to me, and yet I can judge them just as if they were someone else's work. They are a long way away from me, but they are still authentic. They describe a precise period and situation which belong to me. Germans are obstinate, straightforward people. Starting and stopping over and over again is a testing experience.

Woodmen
Waldarbeiter
1968
The Art Institute of Chicago

The period of the 'Heroes' and 'Idols' lasted from 1965 to 1968, or thereabouts?

Yes, from 1964 to 1968.

The 1968 pictures interest me very much. They are pictures with cuts in them, an organization of the image into planes. These pictures seem to be the first onslaught on the integrity of the image, and also, specifically, on that of the symbolic image.

What I did up to 1968 is a body of work that fills up a biography, and I could have stopped there. But there comes a moment when there is nothing more to be got from previous experiences; it's all over. Gradually the idea dawned on me that I could launch myself into painting. I thought that to do a picture I did not necessarily have to have an interesting subject. The object had no intrinsic importance any more. So I chose insignificant things. I painted a cow, a dog, a beautiful landscape; but I never did them from nature, I reinvented them and organized them in the picture in an unaccustomed way. It was an unaccustomed kind of organization because the objects, dogs for instance, were climbing up towards the top of the picture, or else coming down. Or the painting fractured in the middle of one image to start on another. I painted the dog in a completely normal way, I painted half of it and then I broke off, then I started again, and broke off again, and so on. This experience led to the idea that an object hasn't a lot to do with the value and the reality of a painting. It isn't necessary. This is not to say that I do abstract painting. It is just that there is no link, no relationship, between the object and me.

The object expresses nothing. Painting is not a means to an end. On the contrary, painting is autonomous. And I told myself that if this was so I would have to take things that were a traditional part of painting on the level of subject matter – that is to say a landscape, a portrait, a nude – and turn them upside down. This is the best way to empty the content out of what one paints. When one paints a portrait upside down, it is impossible to say: 'This portrait represents my wife, and I gave her a particular expression'. This method leaves no possible room for literary interpretation.

When you went from the early works to the fracture paintings, then to the upside-down pictures, did this have anything to do with current political and social developments?

No, since I left Berlin in 1966 I have lived in total isolation. This isolation was the consequence of the Berlin exhibition and the scandal that followed. I went into the country, to a little village, and had nothing more to do with artists, dealers, and the like. I have never involved myself in politics since, because my experiences in East Germany showed me just how dangerous the influence of a false education can be. I am very suspicious of any political commitment, whatever it may be.

The pictures, that is to say the 'Heroes', existed, and that was enough for me. Then there came another period of my life, and in my isolation I had to get on with something that contained nothing but what was my work. So I did that and nothing else. I thought about my painting and wondered why, of all the pictures in the history of art, one might leave me indifferent and another interest me much more. I pondered on whether, if I like a painting, a picture by Courbet or Degas, for example, this comes from what is depicted, the accuracy of the depiction, or from the imagination, the artistic idea that transcends what is depicted and really makes the picture. When Grünewald paints a *Crucifixion*, for instance, and paints it as well as he does, are we to suppose that this springs from his own religious feeling?

Many people think so. For my part, I think it's a secondary matter.

The fractures and inversions in your paintings are formalist devices, and at that time the issues of formalism loomed large – perhaps too large – in European and American painting. Can you trace a link between these works and the preoccupations that were then current?

We've mentioned Dadaism, and it is time to talk about someone who took Dadaism a stage forward, just as Schwitters did. I mean Rauschenberg, his first works. I've seen these works only in reproduction, and to me they seem very dependent on Schwitters. From the artistic point of view, I have never compared them to my own situation, my own works. Even if other artists have concerned themselves with the same issues as I have, their situation is different from mine. I cannot make reference to them under any circumstances. The motifs I used in my first upside-down paintings exist in traditional paintings, portraits, nudes and landscapes; there exists, for example, a painting by Ferdinand von Rayski, *Pause During a Hunt in the Wärmsdorferwald,* which I did some work on and turned upside-down. And as early as the 1960s I started painting figurative pictures of my own inspired by Ferdinand von Rayski's works. These are the famous 'Rayski Heads' of the 1960s. The fact that I quoted from Rayski is proof that I was independent of what was then being done elsewhere. For Rayski is an unknown artist.

When did you paint the Pause During a Hunt in the Wärmsdorferwald?

In 1969.

In the Nationalgalerie in Berlin there's a painting by Max Beckmann called Death...

Yes, I know it. I could never get along with Beckmann and the other Expressionists. I didn't like all that. Later on, I started to think about it. Even then, people were starting to say that my works had a link with German Expressionism. In fact this only applies to the way I handle the canvas, my manual use of the canvas. I have never had any relationship with Expressionism. In fact I have always wondered why it was so alien to me. The reason is that the Expressionists use a method that illustrates our environment, the world we live in. They use what exists; they extract from it an illustrative method of making a painting. Everything is linked. Painting a cow green doesn't necessarily entail losing touch with one's environment. I have always invented the objects and the various figurations that I wanted to show. I have never had a model. That is something that has remained entirely alien to me, something that does not suit me at all.

No models, but conventional subjects?

Motifs, yes. It was just because they were conventional that they were valid and possible. When I set out to paint a portrait, I didn't need to paint two noses, four eyes or other distortions. I could tackle the portrait like a photograph, and then turn it upside down afterwards. I had no need of the expressiveness that is considered to be a necessary part of a painting and of a portrait.

Let's look more closely at the words 'conventional' and 'traditional'. Does the fact of being cut off from one's original roots and from one's family, with all that that implies, mean that the individual has to find a whole system of roots within the world he has chosen, which is that of painting, and for example to work on developing these traditional themes?

I don't see things that way. There is an important point involved, but it's a personal issue, a question of character. Germans in general, and I in particular, need to have a reason for everything we do. This reason has to be very clear to me. I am not going to do anything just for fun, or as an experiment. I can do nothing, as an artist, to change the world around me. Neither to make it more beautiful nor to make it uglier. There are artists who do, however. They take an object and give it new forms.

That is a method, again, that is linked to the idea of illustrating the world. And I just can't do that.

Every time I see something like that, I say to myself that it's like Matisse all over again. It's something I don't understand.

Just now we were talking about Matisse. His virtual obsession with painting interiors, or Picasso's with painting portraits of his wife, is a way of structuring painting and neutralizing it in time, so that all that is left is expressiveness.

Everything I do, and everything I think has just one purpose: to enable me to paint a picture.

There is no other reason.

How did you get the idea of doing sculptures?

The Venice Biennale was an opportunity to put an idea into practice through sculpture. I think that sculpture is a more direct way than painting to approach the same issue, because sculpture is more primitive, more brutal, and lacks the reserve that you find in painting. I was confirmed in this idea by the violence of controversy raised by my Venice sculpture. There is a different kind of work involved, of course: physical work. It's a problem; all sculptors do less work than painters, but they need a different sort of strength, a different power.

I have always taken things that have been worked on already and added a new aspect to them. Engraving, for example. Engraving is a specialized thing. Collectors of prints and drawings are like stamp-collectors; it's very intimate, highly personal. I started off by making very small works, and the one day I did an engraving that completely broke the mould, because it was 1.5 metres, five feet high. There is a tradition of engraving, and the way I practise it places me right outside that tradition. It's more or less the same thing that happened with sculpture. When I started doing sculpture, I was able to negotiate with that tradition.

For instance, sculpture is one thing in Europe, another in Africa, another in Asia, and so on. So I thought about the tradition of sculpture in Africa. It interested me very much. When one thinks of primordial form in sculpture, one always thinks of sculpture from Africa, because in Europe there are not many examples of this kind of sculpture. In Germany, for instance, there are not many examples of the sculpture that was being done three thousand years ago. Near here, on the moor, they've found two sculptures of idols which are relics of a period no one knows anything about. Did you know about them?

No.

They are two specimens that are impossible to localize. They could be from Africa, from Egypt or from the Pacific. They are a pair of very large wooden idols, a man and a woman. The figuration, the pattern of the outline, are stereotyped. The same thing happens in African sculpture. In Africa there are many tribes, and every one of them has its own sculptural structures that can be very clearly distinguished even when different tribes live very close together. One wonders why. One is asking oneself that question, if one compares our present-day sculpture with the works that were made in Europe three or four thousand years ago and continue to be made in Africa.

I have found an explanation, which has to do with the artist, with his desire to make a sculpture. In Africa, the work of an artist, a sculptor, is done for just one reason. The sculpture is needed for a specific purpose; and being made of wood it decays very quickly. It is always having to be done over again, having to be reproduced. This way of

Model for a Sculpture
1979/80
Museum Ludwig, Cologne
Photographed at Derneburg

wanting to conserve sculpture has nothing to do with the motivation we have in Europe. We make a sculpture or a painting *against* a sculpture or a painting that someone else has made before us; always *against* something. We can't work as sculptors against other people without destroying other people's work. Because sculptures and paintings in Europe are things that are present, we can relate to all the sculptures that have been done in Europe over the last eight hundred years. In Africa this issue doesn't arise. There are sculptures that people have been making for several thousand years and which are constants – even when they are brand-new, even when they were made yesterday. The reason is that to them the father, the ancestor, is not an enemy. The artist's relationship to his work does not exist, so all there is to do is to remake something. If you consider several millennia of civilization in the Congo, for example, and look at a single figure that has been standardized over the entire period, there is hardly any difference. There is some talk of degeneration, but it is minimal, just details.

Basically, all these sculptures bear the mark of a high culture. They are a long way from natural form. They are inventions. A model has been devised which can stand for

Derneburg
1982

a god, or an ancestor, and people wonder why. One can think of many artists who have been fascinated by these very basic forms: Picasso, Braque, Kirchner, Schmidt-Rottluff. They all took these unfamiliar things that come from Cameroun, or Gabon, and appreciated the element of something 'never before seen' that is in them. For my part, this is the issue that concerns me too. I am not interested in adopting the elevated cultural vantage-point of European sculpture and making use of all its sophisticated refinements in order to 'improve' on anything. That's a situation I loathe. Whenever I start a painting I set out to formulate things as if I were the first one, the only one, and as if all the precedents did not exist; even though I know that there are thousands of precedents ranged against me. One has always to think of *making* something, something valid. That is my life.

I'd like to talk about the attitudes of your figures. The first sculpture, the Venice one, has one arm raised. There are other figures, too, with a one-sided gesture. How did you get the ideas for the attitudes of your sculptures?

It comes from signs. When you have a sign, a cross or whatever, it has its origin – a real, not an abstract origin – in a human posture. When someone takes up an extreme posture the expression, in the sense of a sign, is more obvious. For instance, to make an elephant or a tiger, the best way is to imitate the posture of an elephant or a tiger with one's human body. In China there is a concentration exercise in which you imitate certain animals in their movements and their expressions, starting with the face and going on to the whole body. You turn yourself into a snake, a tiger, or an elephant. This extreme situation into which you can transpose yourself is one that interests me very much indeed, on account of its charge. For instance, the arm gestures, the salutes, that we have talked about, are extreme postures that look abstract, that are highly artistic, are highly charged with meaning, but are never thought through. Everyone knows how powerful they can be.

When I make sculptures or paintings, I adopt similar attitudes. I don't follow the well-trodden path. When one sits down to do a drawing, one's inclination is to do it in a very harmonious way. I hate that. I just don't like it at all. I can only get my artistic result by breaking away from the harmonious drawing, by being very attentive, highly disciplined, and aware that I am working against all that, that I am going against the grain.

This avoidance of symmetry is something I have been working with for a long time; I was doing this when I painted the fracture paintings. When I took up a piece of wood, it wasn't because I wanted to go along with the piece of wood but to confront the piece of wood. This is working against the grain, and it applies to all the fields in which I operate: drawing, painting, structure, colour, texture. In this whole quest I need some kindred spirits; it's pleasant to find the Northern European sculptures we were just talking about, for instance.

On the wall of your sculpture studio there are a number of drawings. This leads me to ask you: can you define the relationship between your painting and your sculptures?

There is another question. The pictures I do, I turn upside-down. I do the same with the drawings, but not the sculptures. The only way I can do a painting or a drawing is to do it upside-down. With the sculptures, it's different. The fact that a sculpture is not upside-down does not mean that what I am doing is different, but that for me the method is not a form of artistic speculation but the possibility of doing what I want to do. I don't make a sculpture by thinking of the volume as concave, then suddenly deciding to make it convex, or by any other such thought. That sort of speculative approach doesn't exist, it isn't possible. The way sculpture can be made is different, and simpler. I think that what makes it possible to do what I do is the method of direct aggression.

Is this why your working technique is very much tied to drawing into the block with a saw and marking the design in negative with paint, as in an engraving?

Yes, thus there is the surface of a sculpture; for me it is closely related to the drawings I've done. The tool is the same, and so is the colour. For instance, I can put down a colour that will emphasize the act I am performing. I can put that down. I don't use green, blue or black, unless I know why. The lines I trace on a sculpture are identical to those on drawing.

Could we talk about the heads? Could you explain the differences between the heads? What are the ideas that led to these different sculptures? What do you mean these heads to say?

The first paintings I did with a configuration, or let's say with a concrete image, the first ones that were concrete in my mind – not those that were inspired by tachist images or school images – were not heads, in the sense of portraits, but something like an image which has in the centre, in the thick of a soup of colours, a head which became more and more distinct from one painting to the next. If you ask a lay person to do a drawing, I think he'll do a head, because the head, from the formal point of view, is not a very rich thing. It's easy to do. You can do a round ball. And when I do heads in sculpture, the same thing happens as when I was painting heads in 1960. The way to set out to turn an idea into reality, the simplest way, is to do a head. In sculpture, it's exactly the same thing: the head is never a portrait, it's quite simply the vehicle of my artistic ideas.

Do you know the sculptures that painters like De Kooning, for example, have been doing recently?

Yes, I've seen some of them.

I think De Kooning is a very good painter, and I find his sculptures very strange, visually perplexing, because they don't correspond to the form of sculpture that we know. They don't respect the principles of sculpture. They have no muscles, no skeletons, no skin. They only have a surface without content.

He works the clay or the plaster like dabs of paint.

Derneburg
1982

Yes, but his paintings are magnificent. They satisfy all the criteria of painting. His sculptures, on the other hand, do not satisfy any of the criteria of sculpture. But they are fantastic, very different, highly surprising.

There are other painters who do sculpture, too. Do you know Dodeigne? He's done a lot of sculptures. If you compare them with paintings you can say that they are things that have volume. They have enormous brutality, enormous volume.

Dodeigne works in stone. Why have you chosen to work in wood?

By working in wood, I want to avoid all manual dexterity, all artistic elegance, every-thing to do with construction. I don't want to construct anything.

Since we were talking about Dodeigne he didn't do any constructing either!

Derneburg
1982

I mentioned him because I wanted an example of someone who is at the opposite pole from De Kooning. He uses a material which is generally employed to construct things, but his talent has enabled him to produce things that are highly *de*structive. You won't find one line in his sculpture that conveys harmony or repose. These things are spectres, but that is something we need.

Could we come back to the role of line in your sculpture?

There are certain peoples who have tattoos, for instance, or body paintings; Levi-Strauss has done some work on this. Among peoples who have no painting or sculpture, there exists a form of body-painting which completely transforms the body by applying asymmetrical designs to it. For instance, they paint a line and then a circle, one big eye and one little one, dots on one side and an elaborate design on the other, and this goes on all over the body. Your body is distorted by forms of articulation that clash, with no harmony to them at all. It happens in Indonesia and the Amazon Basin.

The fact is that a symmetrical face is boring and an asymmetrical one is surprising and interesting. It produces a shock at first, and then you look closer and start to make out an order underlying the asymmetry – a system. It is interesting, you see, to break up the symmetry that we all have, and this is an artistic method.

I have been struck by one characteristic that is common to a number of the African figurines in your collection. All these figures are making big gestures, which is something that I think is rather rare in African sculpture. What led you to bring these pieces together?

Yes, that's true, it is unusual. But that's just what interests me, because it departs from the norm. These sculptures, in the place where they were made, have no normal, ordinary functions – no – they have extreme functions. The movement of dolls, their dynamics, the way their movement is carried to an extreme, provides a model for this. A lot of dolls had these same positions. There are two peoples, two ethnic groups, that make dolls like this. When a chief dies they make a doll and put the body inside it, and so the body mummifies. The doll, when it is sewn up – it's made of cloth – is 4 to 5 metres, 13 to 16 feet high. It is always in the same posture. Afterwards they burn it. Later they make little ones, all of which have the same size and the same posture, and which are marked with the body painting and the emblems that were proper to the chief. There is nothing arbitrary about all this, it is not an artist's idea, but it is a model to follow.

Your interest in images that serve as models and at the same time go back to origins: is this what guides you in working out the positions of your sculptures?

Yes, I'm curious; I find that very interesting.

And then, you have to try to understand the reason for this interest in origins. You have to understand where the fascination with these images comes from. All the examples of African sculpture that exist, even the simplest of them, are worked on with great precision, and yet you never see any traces of the work that has gone into them. What you see is always a piece of work done with great precision, with the purpose of giving an extreme form of bodily expression to what we would call insanity. When something is done with that much precision, it has a certain value, a certain importance.

Although the sculptor's hand is highly visible in your sculptures, it doesn't seem to reflect the way in which you have used it. Usually, when there is a pronounced gestural element in a work, it emphasizes the material nature of the making of the work, but in your sculptures and paintings one doesn't have this impression at all.

Yes, I can see what you are getting at. My sculptures and paintings give the impression that the gestural element, rapidity of movement, plays an important part in them, but in fact it doesn't. I work with fragments. I love fragmentary things.

Has this fragmentation anything to do with the fact that you have several studios and can work on several different works at the same time?

Actually I don't move about a lot. It sometimes happens that I am working on several paintings concurrently, but mostly I work on one thing at a time, the orange, or the man in bed, for example. There is very little variation in the colour, or in the pose of a given figure, a few minimal variations at most. My work never deals with a wide range of themes. It's all very narrow, with me.

So you never work on several series or types of works at the same time?

No. For instance, if I'm making sculpture, I can't paint at the same time. When I make sculpture, I make *one* sculpture, and maybe I start on another, but then the sculptures resemble each other. If they were different, it would mean that I had decided to deal with more than one subject, to tell more than one story.

Perhaps this explains the wide divergences between the Venice sculpture, the sculpture with a spherical body, and the latest sculptures, which are three forms of salutation.

The Venice sculpture has gone through a number of transformations. This sculpture that I have drawn was one of the successive states of the Venice sculpture. I had this state in my mind, I had it as a schematic idea, but I could not get anywhere with it. Then, after the Venice work was finished, I took up this same project again, two years later, and still I got nowhere. I worked on the same idea for three years. Now I have set the sketch aside, and I have to say that it's a bad one, a reflection of a moment of weakness, because it reveals the impossibility of making sculpture in a single block. It needs a number of pieces and a number of woods assembled together. It can't be made in one piece. I didn't know what sort of line I could extract from one single block, so I combined several fragments in this sketch. But it's a sketch for a retreat. It's not an offensive plan but a defensive one. Now, with the much simpler results I have obtained, I am much happier. I said at the time, in Venice, that it was a model for a sculpture. I never said it was a sculpture. It's a model, an idea for a sculpture. This assemblage of several elements is a very defensive thing.

Derneburg
1986

Talking about this head yesterday, you were saying that it came from a long way away, but you also talked about the discord there was between a sculpture like this one – the figure with arm raised – and the stooping figure which came before it, and which you didn't like. One seemed to be closer to your idea of comtemporary sculpture than the other.

It's no different from painting.

What I make can be a gesture or a pose for a figure. What is decisive about this gesture, from the iconographic point of view – the raised arm, the stooping back, the bent head, the open eyes, or the open mouth – is that all these are attitudes that need no interpretation. When sculpture is made, it has to be like painting, it has to be a total invention in the sense of being independent of natural forms. The issue is simply form. It is present in sculpture, but then it has nothing to do with nature.

Derneburg
1986

What went on when you were working on this stooping figure, in the idea of making it and the difficulty of creating it?

The work starts in a similar way to the paintings. It is not a process of analysis but an act of aggression. That is the basis of the work. What I make is figurative, but I can't imagine that it would be any different if it wasn't figurative. Nevertheless this figuration is independent of any control, or of any link with a real example or a real fact. This is equally so when it comes to interpreting the meaning. If I raise one arm, as in the Venice sculpture for example, this does not mean that someone is saluting in the German fashion; it's a movement which constitutes a sign within the evolutionary development of iconography, and which has a number of different meanings depending on its origin. The meanings make their appearance only because the posture of the sculpture is clear and unequivocal in its design.

Still on the subject of this black sculpture: you detected a discrepancy between the head and the body, and you were saying that the head was too realistic.

I would say that it's super-bourgeois. It has a gesture, it has a posture, but it's small. It's not an extreme posture. It's mean. It's too close to something that's already known. I don't know what, exactly, but I'm suspicious. It's not formalistic enough at the moment, but it will get better...

Could you talk about this orange head?

It's crazy, all right. It's hard to say. I think it's like the orange-eaters. It's a head with big eyes and a big mouth, but it's far removed from this other head, for instance, like a mad invention – the way a child might have made it. It has a certain speed about it. It looks like a head from Easter Island. It has always been like that, and I didn't like it at all, but suddenly I had the idea of adding colour and working on it a bit more, and it turned into something like a drawing, like a mad person's drawing. I tucked in the chin, I made the eyes bigger...

What governs your choice of expression?

What I do is always something extreme: in the dimensions, the work, the unfolding of the action and the representation. Even when I make a closed mouth or open eyes, I am doing something extreme. In order to represent extremes of this sort, I need lines, lines in discord. Without this control I can never find a way out. It's not enough just to make a particular gesture.

The paint on the orange head doesn't look damaged by subsequent work on the wood, as it does in other sculptures.

That's the way it came. When I start work, most of the time, I coat my sculpture with paint. When it's covered with black, the sculpture has no shadow, no volume, no sculptural quality; and as I work I can keep a better check on what is going on. That is where colour starts. Finally, with the same aggressiveness in my use of colour, I do significant things with it in the final representation. These things are important. If it doesn't work I strip it off, as I do in my paintings. I cut the wood away and put the paint back on. There is only one head that has no colour on it.

Do you draw with the saw?

In sculpture, using the saw is an aggressive process which is the equivalent of drawing. It's a linear signal. For example, when you can see the ribs, this hasn't got an anatomical significance, it's not justified by anatomy, but it is a fascination that gives life to the body.

Derneburg 1983

SCULPTURE

Untitled
1979/80
Lime wood, with blue and black tempera
25½ x 15½ x 16½ in; 65 x 39 x 42 cm

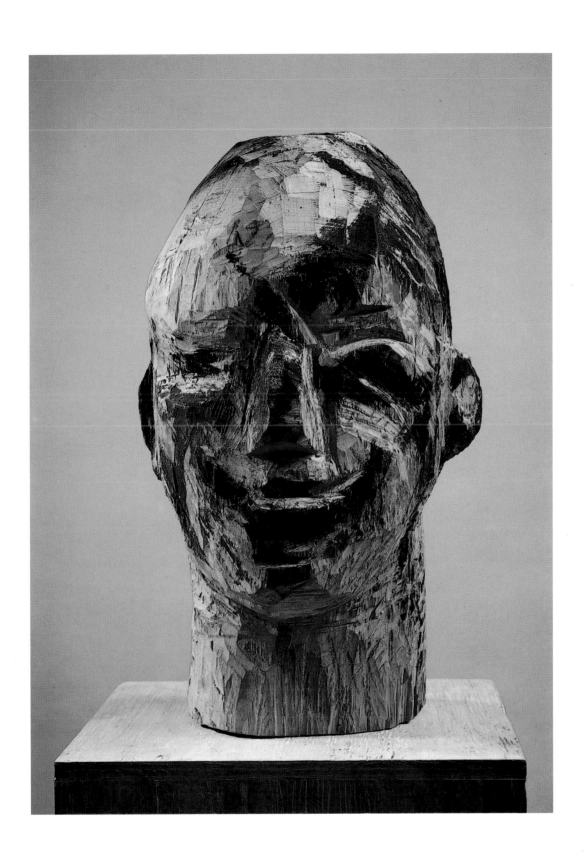

Untitled
1979/80
Beech, with red-brown oil paint
22 x 17¾ x 18 in; 56 x 45 x 46 cm

Untitled
1982
Beech
19¾ x 17¾ x 17¾ in; 50 x 45 x 45 cm

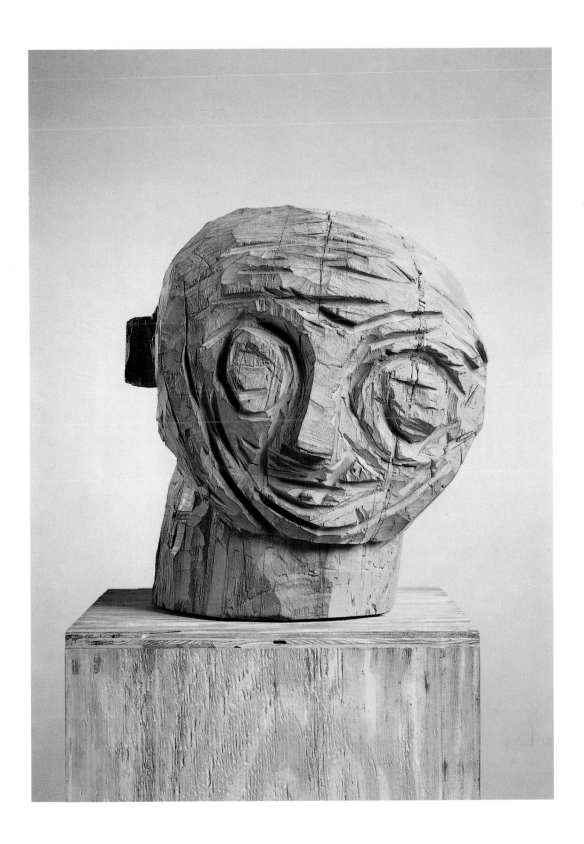

Greetings from Oslo
Gruss aus Oslo
1986
Lime wood, with charcoal and red oil paint
89½ x 21½ x 10½ in; 227 x 54.5 x 27 cm

Greetings from Oslo
Gruss aus Oslo
1986
(detail)

EARLY WOODCUTS

Alfred Rethel's *Dance of Death* prints were the first woodcuts I saw. The Romantic idea and the box of bricks, cold and enmeshed by double outline and stencil; the nursery is all part of it.

After that came the *Life of the Virgin*, the woodcut technique, and later the *Woman on the Brink*. This was a hierarchy that cried out for me to do something disruptive. I introduced the soul.

I exploited the sentimental pose of the inward-turning eyes, although of course I know that the shaving raised by the gouge is first the white drop, then the tear: Mourning, the sinking form. Sign for woman. In spite of that, it is necessary to counter technique with soul. And so, among many other things, I have done Richard Wagner as a woman.

Georg Baselitz
Derneburg 22 June 1986

Partisan
1966
Catalogue no 1b

2. Zustand   Grieke 66

L. R.
1966
Catalogue no 2a

Untitled
1966
Catalogue no 3b

Large Head
Grosser Kopf
1966
Catalogue no 4b

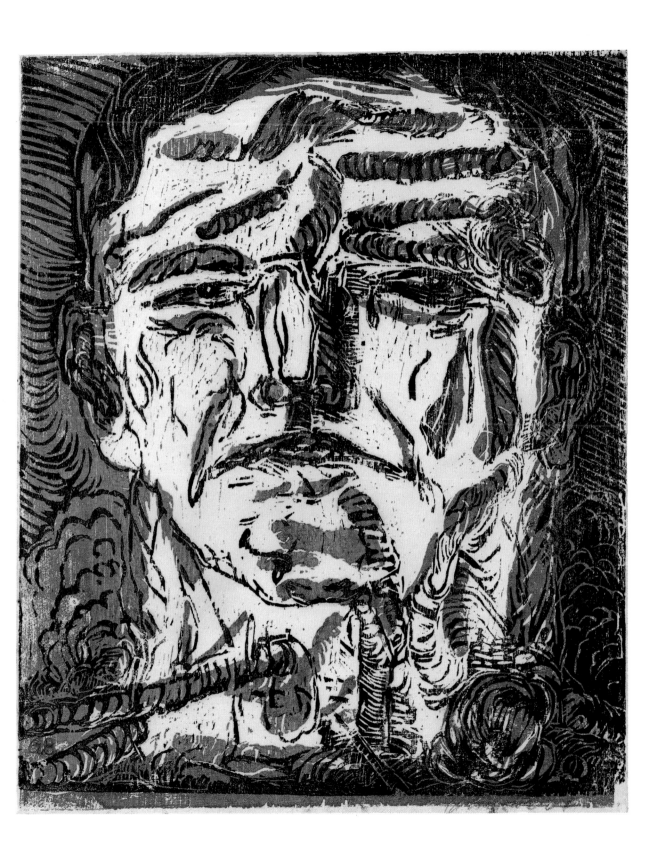

Untitled
1967
Catalogue no 5b

1. Zustand 3 Platten 4 Abzüge   1/4   [signature] 67

Catalogue of Early Woodcuts

1 **Partisan**
1966
Woodcut
Block: 14¼ x 11¾ in; 36.2 x 30 cm

a Printed from one block in black/brown ink on smooth
off-white wove paper, 17 x 13½ in; 43 x 34.5 cm
Signed and dated in pencil (at lower right): *Baselitz 66*
Inscribed in pencil (at lower left): *2. Zustand*
Proof before the edition of about 15 in this state
Jahn 45 ii/111

b Printed from two blocks in black and grey/blue ink on
ivory laid paper, 15 x 12½ in; 38.1 x 32 cm
Signed and dated in pencil (at lower right): *Baselitz 66*
Inscribed in pencil (at lower left): *2. Zustand*
Proof before the edition of about 15 in this state
Jahn 45 ii/111

c Printed from three blocks in black, grey/brown and ochre
ink on ivory laid paper, 15 x 12½ in; 38.1 x 32 cm
Signed and dated in pencil (at lower right): *Baselitz 66*
Inscribed in pencil (at upper left verso): *3. Zustand 66*
Proof before the edition of 20 in this state
Jahn 45 iii/111

2 **L. R.**
   1966
   Woodcut
   Block: 16½ x 13 in; 42 x 33 cm

a Printed from three blocks in black, grey/green and
   ochre ink on stiff wove paper with 'Schoeller/Turm'
   blindstamp at lower right, 17 x 13⅛ in; 43 x 33.5 cm
   Signed and dated in pencil (at lower right verso):
   Baselitz 66
   One of an edition of about 20 colour variants in this
   state
   Jahn 49 ii/111

b Printed from three blocks in black, grey/green and
   purple ink on ivory laid paper, 17¾ x 13¾ in; 45 x 35 cm
   Signed and dated in pencil (at lower right): *Baselitz 66*
   One of an edition of about 20 colour variants in this
   state
   Jahn 49 ii/111

c Printed from three blocks in black, grey/green and
   grey ink on stiff wove paper with 'Schoeller/Turm'
   blindstamp at lower right, 17¼ x 13¼ in; 44 x 34 cm
   Signed and dated in pencil (at lower right): *Baselitz 66*
   One of an edition of about 20 colour variants in this
   state
   Jahn 49 ii/111

d Printed from three blocks in black, grey/green and light green ink on stiff wove paper with 'Schoeller/Turm' blindstamp at lower right, 17¾ x 13¼ in; 45 x 34 cm
Signed and dated in pencil (at lower right): *Baselitz 66*
One of an edition of about 20 colour variants in this state
Jahn 49 ii/III

3 **Untitled**
1966
Woodcut
Block: 16½ x 13 in; 42 x 33 cm

a Printed from one block in black ink on ivory laid paper with 'PLBA' watermark, 18⅞ x 15¾ in; 48 x 40 cm
Signed and dated in pencil (at lower right): *Baselitz 66*
Proof before the edition of about 15 colour variants in the final state
Jahn 50 ii or iii/III

b Printed from two blocks in black and light green ink on off-white wove paper with 'FABRIANO' watermark, 17 x 13⅛ in; 43 x 33.5 cm
Signed and dated in pencil (at lower right verso): *Baselitz 66*
One of an edition of about 15 colour variants in this state
Jahn 50 iii/III

4　**Large Head**
Grosser Kopf
1966
Woodcut
Block: 18¾ x 16 in; 47.5 x 40.5 cm

a　Printed from two blocks in black and grey/green ink
with monotype inking on off-white laid paper
19 x 16⅛ in; 48.5 x 41 cm
Proof before the edition of about 20 colour variants in
the final state
Jahn 54 i or ii/11

b　Printed from two blocks in black and olive green ink on
smooth off-white wove paper painted with gouache on
recto before printing and with a fragment of an
unrecorded lithograph on verso, 19 x 16⅛ in;
48.5 x 41 cm
Signed and dated in pencil (at lower right): *Baselitz 68*
Initialled in pencil (within image at lower left): *G.B.*
Signed and dated in pencil (at upper centre verso):
G. Baselitz 68
One of an edition of about 20 colour variants in this
state
Jahn 54 ii/11

c　Printed from two blocks in black and olive green ink on
smooth off-white wove paper over-painted with
gouache and watercolour on recto and with a fragment
of an unrecorded lithograph on verso, 19⅛ x 16 in;
48.7 x 40.6 cm
Signed and dated in pencil (at lower right): *Baselitz 67*
Inscribed in pencil (at upper centre verso):
Baselitz 67/Kopf
One of an edition of about 20 colour variants in this
state
Jahn 54 ii/11

5 **Untitled**
   1967
   Woodcut
   14⅛ x 11¾ in; 36 x 30 cm

a Printed from one block in black ink on off-white laid
   paper, 20 x 14 in; 50.5 x 35.5 cm
   Signed and dated in pencil (at lower right): *Baselitz 67*
   Proof before the edition of about 20 colour variants in
   this state
   Jahn 55 i/v

b Printed from three blocks in black, purple, and light
   brown ink on off-white laid paper, 14¾ x 12⅜ in;
   37.5 x 31.5 cm
   Signed and dated in pencil (at lower right): *Baselitz 67*
   Inscribed in pencil (at lower left): *1. Zustand 3 Platten
   4 Abzuge ¹/4*
   Proof before the edition of about 20 colour variants in
   this state
   Jahn 55 i/v

c Printed from three blocks in black, violet, and light
   green ink on off-white laid paper with 'Ingres Canson
   – France' watermark, 15½ x 12¾ in; 39 x 32.5 cm
   Signed and dated in pencil (at lower right): *Baselitz 67*
   One of an edition of about 20 colour variants in this
   state
   Jahn 55 i/v

d Printed from two blocks in black and brick red ink on off-white laid paper with 'Ingres Canson – France' watermark, 16⅛ x 13 in; 41 x 33 cm
Signed and dated in pencil (at lower right): *Baselitz 67*
One of four or five proofs in this state
Jahn 55 iii/v

References to Fred Jahn *Baselitz: Werkverzeichnis der Druckgrafic, Band I, 1963-1974* Verlag Gachnang & Springer, Berlin 1983, are abbreviated to 'Jahn.'

We would like to express our grateful thanks to Georg and Elke Baselitz, Daniel Blau, David Britt, Balthasar Burkhard, Jean-Louis Froment, Detlev Gretenkort, Hans Dieter Henke, Jochen Littkemann, Helen van der Meij, Jean-Marc Poinsot, Norman Rosenthal, and Michael Werner.

Exhibition 2 December to 16 January 1988

Interview translated by David Britt

PHOTOGRAPHIC CREDITS

Sculpture
J Littkemann

Woodcuts
Prudence Cuming Associates

Frontispiece and studio portraits 1986
Daniel Blau

Studio photographs 1982
Balthasar Burkhard

Other text reproductions
*Hess. Landesmuseum, Darmstadt;
J. Littkemann; Prudence Cuming
Associates; Bernd-Peter Keiser*

ISBN 0 947564 13 6

Catalogue designed by Simon Rendall
and printed by Elbracht & Co